People of the Ancient World

THE
VIKINGS

WRITTEN BY
VIRGINIA SCHOMP

Franklin Watts
A Division of Scholastic Inc.
New York Toronto London Auckland Sydney
Mexico City New Delhi Hong Kong
Danbury, Connecticut

For Jonathan Paul Martin

Note to readers: Definitions for words in bold can be found in the Glossary at the back of this book.

The "Head Ransom" poem from *Egil's Saga* (page 79) was translated by Bernard Scudder.

Photographs © 2005: akg-Images, London: 75 (Schutze/Rodemann), 30; Art Resource, NY: 60 (Werner Forman), 82 top left, 83, 86, 87 (Erich Lessing), 26 (The British Museum); Bridgeman Art Library International Ltd., London/New York: 93, 96 bottom (Arnamagnaen Collection, Denmark), 78, 96 center (Arni Magnuson Institute, Reykajavik, Iceland), 89, 95 bottom right, 99 bottom (Philip Mould, Historical Portraits Ltd., London, UK), 70 (Nationalmuseum, Stockholm, Sweden), 13, 92 right, 97 bottom (Royal Library, Copenhagen, Denmark), 49 (Viking Ship Museum, Oslo Norway); Corbis Images: 64 (Archivo Iconografico, S.A.), 69, 95 left, 96 top (Bettmann), 37 (Richard T. Nowitz), 4 center, 9, 10, 16, 57, 59, 88 top left (Ted Spiegel), 56 (Nik Wheeler); Folio, Inc./Walter Bibikow: 51; North Wind Picture Archives: 22, 39, 41; Robertstock.com: 42 (G. Ahrens), 15; Sovfoto/Eastfoto: 62; Stock Montage, Inc.: 94, 98 bottom; The Art Archive/Picture Desk: 76 (Dagli Orti), 17, 97 top (Dagli Orti/National Museum Copenhagen), 46 (Dagli Orti/Oldsaksammlung, Oslo), 33; The Image Works: 29 (The British Museum/Topham-HIP), 53, 66 (Topham), 81, 99 (Topham Picturepoint); The Museum of National Antiquities, Stockholm Sweden/Christer Ahlin: 47; TRIP Photo Library: 98 top (I Corse), 7, 92 left (Douglas Houghton), 32, 36 (J. Ringland); Werner Forman Archive, Ltd.: 27 (Statens Historiska Museum Stockholm), 20 (Thjodminjasafn, Reykajavik, Iceland), 44 (Universitetets Oldsaksamling, Oslo).

Cover art by Dan Andreasen
Map by XNR Productions Inc.

Library of Congress Cataloging-in-Publication Data

Schomp, Virginia.
        The Vikings / Virginia Schomp. — 1st ed.
        p. cm. — (People of the ancient world)

Includes bibliographical references and index.
ISBN 0–531–12382–0 (lib. bdg.) 0–531–16849–2 (pbk.)
1. Vikings—Juvenile literature. 2. Civilization, Viking—Juvenile literature. I. Title. II. Series.

DL65.S385 2005
948'.022—dc22

2004024311

Contents

LEGENDS AND HISTORY

WHAT DO YOU THINK OF WHEN YOU HEAR
the word "Vikings"? Perhaps you picture fierce barbarians in
horned helmets, sailing in long wooden ships to raid distant shores.
This popular image of the Vikings is one-sided and not completely
accurate. It comes mainly from hostile accounts written by their enemies. It is true that the Vikings were
fearsome fighters, but there was much more to their
culture than warfare and piracy. These adventurous
men and women were also highly skilled traders,
explorers, farmers, craftworkers, and poets.

The Vikings' homeland was the area of northern
Europe known as Scandinavia, which includes
present-day Sweden, Norway, and Denmark. Scandinavia is a vast land made up of two peninsulas and
hundreds of islands. From very early times, its people built sturdy wooden boats to travel the inland
waterways and the surrounding seas. Scandinavian

merchants sailed cargo ships to trading centers along the coasts of western Europe. There they heard tales of undefended Christian **monasteries** overflowing with silver and gold. In the late eighth century A.D., Scandinavian raiders set sail for these tempting targets. They rode in **longships,** the finest and fastest vessels the world had ever seen.

Historians traditionally date the beginning of the Viking Age to 793. That was the year of the Scandinavians' first recorded raid, on Lindisfarne, a tiny island off the northeastern coast of England. The monastery of Lindisfarne was one of the holiest sites in the British Isles. Its unarmed monks were no match for the brutal invaders. According to historical accounts, the Scandinavians poured from their ships like wild men, howling and waving swords. Tearing through the settlement, they slaughtered some of the monks and captured others to sell into slavery. They ransacked the buildings and carried off a treasure trove of silver cups, gold crosses, and jewels pried from sacred shrines. "Never before has such terror appeared in Britain," wrote English clergyman and scholar Alcuin, "nor was it thought that such an inroad from the sea could be made. Behold the church . . . spattered with the blood of the priests of God, despoiled of all its ornaments."

Over the next few decades, small bands of Scandinavian warriors staged hit-and-run raids on monasteries and seaports along the coasts of England, Ireland, Scotland, Frisia (the modern-day Netherlands), and Frankia (France and western Germany). Raiding parties struck in the warm summer months, the easiest time for sea travel. Swooping down from their swift ships, they killed and looted. Then they disappeared back over the waters. Europeans lived in terror of the seemingly invincible invaders. They gave the raiders a variety of names, including Danes, Ashmen,

The attack on the monastery at Lindisfarne in 793 signaled the beginning of the Viking Age.

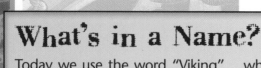

What's in a Name?

Today we use the word "Viking" for all Scandinavians of the late eighth to the mid-eleventh centuries. During the Viking Age itself, however, only adventurers who went raiding earned that title. In Old Norse, the language spoken by the early Scandinavians, the word *víkingr* meant "raider" or "pirate."

heathens, Northmen, and Norsemen. Today we call them Vikings.

Around the middle of the ninth century, the Vikings' tactics changed. Instead of retreating after their attacks, some raiders began to settle in the lands they had looted. Back home in Scandinavia, all the good land was taken. Overseas a bold warrior could carve out a fine new home in captured territory.

By the time the Viking Age ended in the eleventh century, the adventurous Northmen had made a lasting impression. Viking colonies stretched over large areas of western Europe, including parts of England, Ireland, and Normandy (in northern France). Traders and raiders had also ventured east, establishing settlements deep inside what is now Russia. Daring explorers had even crossed the uncharted waters of the North Atlantic Ocean, pushing back the borders of the known world.

For centuries, the Vikings' accomplishments lay buried beneath traditional tales portraying them as brave but bloodthirsty barbarians. In recent years, historians have begun to look deeper. Investigating the lasting traces of the Viking Age, they have searched for the truth behind the legends.

A variety of sources help them in that search. The Vikings

By the 1000s, the Vikings had established colonies throughout much of western Europe. This is a modern-day reconstruction of a traditional Viking village.

themselves left only a few records, mainly messages carved in stone. Most of the written evidence of their activities comes from two very different sources. First, there are the accounts of European churchmen who came into contact with Viking raiders. Second, there are the **sagas,** heroic stories written in Iceland hundreds of years after the Viking Age. Both types of writing are riddled with exaggerations and inventions. However, careful study can uncover many kernels of truth.

Archaeologists uncover the Viking trading center of Hedeby, in what is now Germany. Hedeby was established by Danish raiders and merchants in 808.

To check the accuracy of the written texts, **archaeologists** study the physical remains of the Viking culture. Sifting through the soil of settlements in Scandinavia and abroad, they have uncovered everything from combs and cooking pots to axes and swords. **Artifacts** from Viking villages, cities, and fortresses offer insights into daily life, social organization, and trade. The spectacular

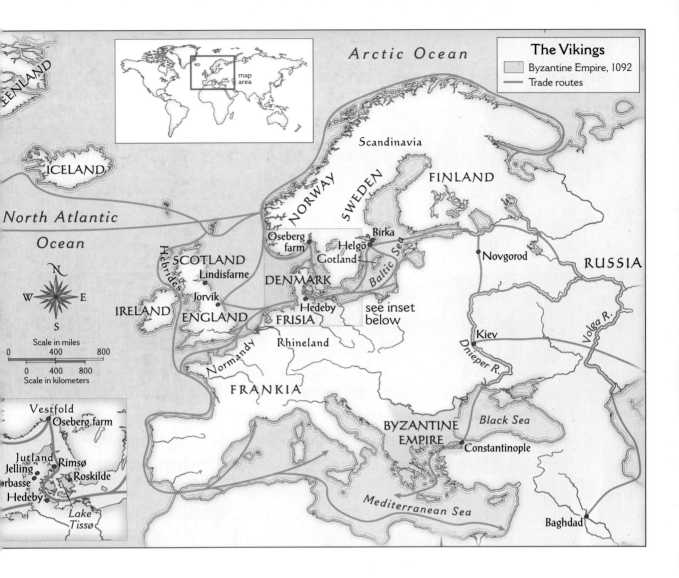

burial mounds of wealthy men and women provide valuable information on the Vikings' beliefs and arts.

Combining evidence from all these different sources, historians have pieced together a complex portrait of the Viking world. Many questions still remain. Today archaeologists continue to search for new clues to add to our knowledge of the Vikings. Their discoveries enrich our understanding of the many ways these remarkable adventurers helped shape our modern world.

Chapter I

WARRIOR KINGS

Harald was just ten years old when he inherited his father's small kingdom in southeast Norway. According to the Icelandic saga *Heimskringla,* or *Chronicle of the Kings of Norway,* he soon grew to become "stout, strong, and manly." One day, the daughter of a neighboring chieftain sneered at the size of his domain. The proud young man made a solemn vow. "Never shall I clip or comb my hair," he said, "until I have subdued the whole of Norway."

To fulfill his "royal words," Harald raised a mighty army. He built a fleet of splendid dragon-headed warships. In one bloody battle after another, he led his forces to victory over his rivals. Finally, Harald defeated a host of enemy chieftains in a great sea battle. With this victory, he became "sole king over all Norway." At a feast celebrating his triumph, the king trimmed his shaggy locks. From then on, he was known as Harald Fairhair, for "all who saw him agreed that . . . he had the most beautiful and abundant head of hair."

Like all Icelandic sagas, *Heimskringla* is a blend of fact and fiction. Other historical sources confirm that Harald Fairhair was a powerful war leader who united most of Norway under

Harald Fairhair greets a visitor in this illustration from a text written in the 1300s.

his rule in the late ninth century. However, we know little about Harald's reign. While the sagas contain many colorful tales, it is sometimes hard to tell which parts are true and which are invented. Still, these time-honored stories are one of our most important sources of information about the warrior kings who ruled the Viking world.

A Chronicle of Kings

Heimskringla was written by Icelandic historian Snorri Sturluson nearly two centuries after the Viking Age. This lively collection of sagas about Norway's Viking kings was based mainly on tales that had been handed down from generation to generation. In the introduction, Snorri defended his choice of sources.

We rest the foundations of our story principally upon the songs which were sung in the presence of the chiefs themselves or of their sons, and take all to be true that is found in such poems about their feats and battles: . . . no one would dare to relate to a chief what he, and all those who heard it, knew to be false and imaginary, not a true account of his deeds; because that would be mockery, not praise.

From Chiefdoms to Kingdoms

Before the Viking Age, Scandinavia was a patchwork of small kingdoms. At the head of each domain was a chieftain. These rich and powerful men owned the largest tracts of land. They surrounded themselves with companies of loyal followers, who stood armed and ready to defend their lands against invaders. To expand their domains, ambitious chieftains sometimes led their warrior bands into battle against neighboring territories. Around the end of the eighth century, many rulers also began to take their men "a-viking," building fame and fortune through raids in foreign lands. The most successful of these bold, adventurous war leaders rose to the rank of king.

In early Viking times, any chieftain who was recognized as lord of all the powerful landowners in a particular domain might call

An ambitious Viking who led his men on daring raids could sometimes win enough wealth, fame, and power to become king.

himself king. Over time, some of these rival kings gained considerably more wealth and influence than others. Large areas of Scandinavia became united under a single strong ruler. The three kingdoms of Denmark, Norway, and Sweden began to emerge.

There is little historical evidence showing exactly how and when the Scandinavian kingdoms were unified. To trace the path from local chieftain to national king, historians begin by studying the written sources. Archaeologists also search for the story of the Viking kings in their building projects and other lasting remains.

Royal Ring Forts

For years, historians were baffled by the remains of five round stone fortresses in Denmark. At first, they thought that the ruins were army barracks built by Svein Forkbeard, who became king of Denmark in 987. Then they used the science of tree-ring dating, or **dendrochronology,** to examine the wood used in the fortress buildings. Each year a tree grows, it forms a growth ring. By studying these rings, dendrochronologists can date old pieces of wood.

Dendrochronology proved that the Danish "ring forts" were built around 980, during the reign of Svein Forkbeard's father, Harald Bluetooth. Historians concluded that Harald built the forts to strengthen his hold on the kingdom. The king stationed soldiers at his royal fortresses to keep an eye on the local population and quickly stamp out signs of rebellion.

Rulers of the Three Kingdoms

No one knows the names of the first kings of Denmark or the extent of the lands they ruled. However, the remains of major public building projects show that Denmark probably had a strong central government before the year 800. One of the most impressive early works was the Danevirke, a massive complex of walls built to guard against invasion from the south.

In the late tenth century, after years of division and civil war, King Harald Bluetooth unified Denmark. Harald's son Svein Forkbeard was a strong war leader who conquered England in 1013. Svein's son Canute the Great took the Danish empire to its greatest glory. Canute ruled over Denmark, Norway, and parts of Sweden, and he was the sole king of England for nearly twenty years.

Norway united more than a century after Denmark, under King Harald Fairhair. Harald's descendants included a parade of bold rulers, beginning with his son Erik Bloodaxe. Erik earned his gruesome nickname by chopping down several of his brothers to secure the throne. The sagas describe him as "a great and fortunate man of war, but badminded, gruff, [and] unfriendly."

King Harald Bluetooth unified Denmark and became its first Christian king.

Harald's grandson Olaf Tryggvason was a famous raider. According to the **Anglo-Saxon Chronicle,** when Olaf's warriors invaded England in 994, they "wrought the greatest harm which any raiding-army could ever do, in burning and raiding and slaughter of men." To prevent further attacks, the English agreed to pay a fortune in **tribute.** A few years later, Olaf's fleet was ambushed by an alliance of his enemies. Outmatched in numbers but not in spirit, the heroic king fought to the last. Then he leaped overboard and sank beneath the sea.

The allies who defeated Olaf Tryggvason included Sweden's king Olof Skötkonung. Olof was the first king known to have ruled both the Götar and the Svear, the two main peoples of Sweden. However, the Swedish kingdom did not become permanently unified until after the Viking Age.

Royal Responsibilities

The most important duties of a Viking king were military. He commanded the armies that defended the kingdom against invasion and guarded the trade routes from piracy. He also organized the building of fortresses and other defenses.

Kings had religious duties, too. The early Vikings were **pagans.** They believed in hundreds of different gods and goddesses. Each of these divine beings presided over a particular area of human existence, such as war, weather, or fertility. There were no full-time pagan priests. Instead, local chieftains led the people in worshiping the gods at different times and places across the country. The king helped secure the gods' favor through the proper observance of rituals, festivals, and sacrifices.

In time, Christianity triumphed over paganism. Christian missionaries first arrived in Scandinavia in the 700s, and some Vikings

Viking Gods and Goddesses

The Vikings believed in a complicated collection of many different gods and goddesses. Here are some of the most important deities, along with their special (often overlapping) areas of responsibility.

Gods

Odin	War, wisdom, learning, magic; patron god of kings, warriors, and poets
Thor	Thunder, lightning, weather, crops; patron god of seamen and farmers
Freyr	Fertility, harvest, rain, wealth, peace
Balder	Sunlight, joy, purity, innocence, beauty
Heimdall	Light, moon; guardian of the bridge leading to the home of the gods
Njord	Sea, winds, fire
Tyr	War, justice
Loki	Mischief, lies

Goddesses

Frigg	Marriage, motherhood, love, fertility; wife of Odin
Freya	Love, fertility, crops; sister of Freyr
Idun	Spring, youth
Hel	Ruler of the realm of the dead

adopted the new faith on their travels abroad. However, Christianity did not really take root until the late tenth century, when it was adopted by the kings.

The Viking kings were probably persuaded to convert to the Christian faith by a combination of sincere beliefs and practical politics. Christianity replaced local worship of the pagan gods with a single faith common to all. That weakened the power of the chieftains and strengthened the central government. Adopting the new religion also improved relations with other Christian kingdoms.

This amulet combines the hammer of the Norse pagan god Thor and the Christian cross.

Qualities of a King

There were no permanent Viking capitals. Instead, most kings owned a network of estates. They visited their royal estates as they toured the kingdom. Accompanying the ruler on his travels was a large household that included his advisers, warriors, and family members.

The royal family often included several wives and many children. Kingship usually passed from father to son, but any man who was descended from a king on either his father's or mother's side could claim the throne. That sometimes led to bloody power

Cruel Conversions

Norway's conversion to Christianity was completed during the reign of Olaf Haraldsson in the early 1000s. Olaf's methods were brutal but effective. According to the *Heimskringla,* a group of Norwegian chieftains once refused to renounce the pagan gods. In response, the king "drove some out of the country, mutilated others of hands or feet, or stung their eyes out; hung up some, cut down some with the sword."

struggles. The losers in these civil wars often went into exile. Many became leaders of Viking raids. Some exiled royals gained enough wealth and power to return home and challenge the established king.

A Viking king's power depended on his ability to attract a band of loyal warriors. He inspired loyalty through his courage and generosity.

Kings were expected to lead their men on daring expeditions that offered a chance to win riches and glory. A good leader fought at the head of his forces. He was fearless in the face of danger. According to the sagas, when advisers urged Norwegian king Magnus Barelegs to be more cautious in battle, he replied in true royal fashion, "Kings are made for honor, not for long life."

Rulers who survived the battlefield could amass a fortune in tribute and **plunder,** or goods taken by force. The ideal king shared the riches. He rewarded his loyal followers with gifts of weapons, land, horses, slaves, and jewelry. He also showed his generosity by treating his men to lavish feasts.

In this imaginative illustration, a skald recites tales of victory and heroic deeds to a group of warriors.

A royal feast could last for several days. It was held in the great hall of a king's estate, which might be decorated with **tapestries** depicting scenes of gods and heroes. The tables were piled high with meat, fish, fruits, vegetables, nuts, and spices. Drinking horns overflowed with beer, wine, and **mead.** The king's men sang and danced to the music of harps, fiddles, flutes, and **pan-pipes.** They played dice and board games, told tall tales of their adventures, and laughed at the antics of the royal jugglers and acrobats.

The highlight of the entertainment was the performance of the **skalds.** These court poets recited verses celebrating the brave deeds and spectacular triumphs of the king and his warriors. A man whose praises were sung in a skaldic poem achieved a kind of immortality. In the words of one poet,

> Cattle die, kinsmen die,
> One day you die yourself;
> But the words of praise will not perish
> When a man wins fair fame.

Chapter II

UPPER-CLASS MEN AND WOMEN

The tenth-century Icelandic poem *Rigsthula* offers a fanciful explanation of how Viking society came to be divided into three classes. A god disguised as a man named Rig wandered the earth. He came to a poor hut, where he spent three days and nights with a ragged old couple. Nine months after the god's visit, the woman gave birth to a coarse, dull-witted boy named Thrall. He was the ancestor of all slaves.

Rig traveled on to a comfortable farmhouse. There he enjoyed the hospitality of a handsome, hardworking couple. Ninth months later, the wife bore a red-cheeked boy called Karl. He was the ancestor of all **freemen.**

Finally, Rig came to a great hall, where he found an elegant couple who offered him fine white bread and silver bowls of wine. Nine months later, the woman delivered a son named Jarl. "Blond was his hair, and bright his cheeks," says the poem. "Grim as a snake's were his glowing eyes." The boy grew up to become an expert rider, hunter, and fighter. "Shields he brandished, bows he shot, and lances [he] wielded." He went to war and conquered many rivals, winning land and treasure. In time, he married the beautiful maiden Erna. They had twelve brave and lordly sons, including the wise warrior Konungr, or "King." From the sons of Jarl and Erna came the upper-class men and women of the Viking world.

Wealth and Power

The Viking upper class included chieftains with a variety of ranks and titles. The lowest-ranking members of this class were the "landed men." They earned their titles by swearing an oath of loyalty to the king and raising a company of warriors for his army. At the top of the social ladder were the *jarls*, or "earls." In early Viking times, there was little difference between these mighty warlords and the kings of small domains. Even after the rise of national kings, the greatest jarls held on to much of their power and independence.

Power came from the control of land and men. High-ranking chieftains owned vast estates that had been in their families for generations. They earned income from their farms, which were worked by **tenant farmers,** hired laborers, servants, and slaves. Many chieftains also collected tribute from lower-ranking freemen. Farmers, merchants, and artisans gave them furs, precious metals, and other goods in return for political and military protection.

Like the kings, Viking chieftains maintained bands of household warriors. A rich lord's loyal followers guarded the peace and collected income in his territories. They also pledged to follow him on raids and other expeditions. One Icelandic saga describes the seasonal adventures of a jarl who kept a band of eighty followers. Each year, this industrious chieftain would take his men "plundering in the **Hebrides** and in Ireland on what he called his 'spring trip.' "

These chess pieces, made from walrus ivory and whales' teeth, depict members of Viking society, including kings, queens, warriors, and Christian bishops. While the figures were crafted around 1150, historians believe that they are fairly accurate examples of clothing and weapon styles toward the end of the Viking Age.

Returning home in late summer, he "stayed till the cornfields had been reaped and the grain was safely in. After that he would go off raiding again. . . . This he used to call his 'autumn trip.' "

Chieftains proudly displayed the wealth they derived from their lands, tribute, and raiding expeditions. Archaeologists exploring the estates of high-ranking Vikings have uncovered great halls decorated with gold, silver, bronze, and ivory treasures. They have also dug up fragments of fine imported glassware. These artifacts are reminders of the grand feasts held by powerful men to advertise their prosperity and cement their bonds with their followers.

Friends of the King

Kings and their followers were bound together by ties of loyalty and obligation. Chieftains pledged to protect the king's interests and carry out his policies in their domains. They also raised troops for the royal army. Some men from powerful families joined the king's warrior band. Others served as royal officials. They might live at court, advising the ruler and representing him on embassies to foreign kingdoms. Officials also were stationed on royal estates or in market towns, where they collected the king's taxes and other income.

In return for all this support, kings handed out generous gifts. Viking poetry often referred to kings as "givers of rings," for the silver and gold arm rings they gave to their

Warriors and other important Vikings might receive arm rings like this one as a reward for their loyalty to the king.

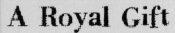
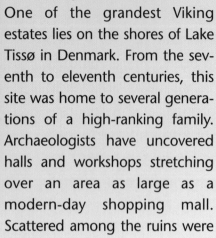

A Royal Gift

One of the grandest Viking estates lies on the shores of Lake Tissø in Denmark. From the seventh to eleventh centuries, this site was home to several generations of a high-ranking family. Archaeologists have uncovered halls and workshops stretching over an area as large as a modern-day shopping mall. Scattered among the ruins were many treasures. There were costly weapons, riding gear, coins, and jewelry. Most valuable of all was a neck ring made of 4.4 pounds (2 kilograms) of gold. In Viking times, it was worth as much as five hundred head of cattle. The ring was probably a present from the king to the lord of the estate, given in return for his support and loyalty.

loyal warriors and other powerful men. One poet wrote this description of the "well-rewarded" followers of King Harald Fairhair.

> By their clothing, their gold armlets
> You see they are the king's friends.
> They bear red cloaks, stained shields,
> Silver-clad swords, ringed mailcoats,
> Gilded sword belts, engraved helmets,
> Rings on their arms, as Harald gave them.

Archaeologists have uncovered evidence of these rich rewards in excavations of estates and graves. Their findings include several valuable swords with two rings forged together on the handle. This image symbolized the oaths sworn between a king and his loyal chieftain.

Honored Wives and Mothers

While Viking society was dominated by men, the women of the upper class enjoyed considerable respect and influence. **Inscriptions** on stones erected in memory of the dead testify to the devotion many Viking men felt for their wives and mothers. One monument in the Danish town of Rimsø is inscribed, "The death of a mother is the worst that can happen to a son." In nearby Jelling (pronounced "yelling"), a memorial stone raised by Harald Bluetooth's father reads, "King Gorm made this monument in memory of Thorvi, his wife, Denmark's **adornment.**"

Further evidence of the high status of women from wealthy families has been found in their graves. In pagan times, high-ranking Vikings were often laid to rest in ships. Their bodies were surrounded by all the practical goods and luxury items they

These oval brooches were found in the grave of a wealthy Viking woman.

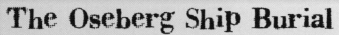

The Oseberg Ship Burial

When archaeologists excavated the burial mound at Oseberg farm in southeast Norway, they knew at once that they had found the grave of a high-ranking Viking. Beneath the mound of earth, clay, and stones were the remains of a longship, buried around 850. A wooden chamber on the ship's deck held two skeletons, probably an upper-class woman and her servant. An abundance of grave goods was included to ensure their comfort in the afterworld. There were sleighs, beds, silk tapestries, oil lamps, frying pans, bowls, and knives. Vessels held a variety of foods, including wild apples, bread dough, walnuts, and spices. There were even two pairs of fine calfskin shoes, specially made for the feet of the older woman.

The Oseberg ship burial was excavated in 1904.

Viking Society

Viking society was divided into three social classes:

Nobles (sometimes called "jarls")	Freemen	*Thralls*
Aristocrats, chieftains, warriors, most skalds (poets)	Farmers, merchants, artisans, hired laborers, servants	Slaves

might need for their journey to the afterworld. Then the ship was buried beneath a huge mound of earth or burned in a blazing funeral **pyre.**

Archaeologists exploring the burial mounds of high-ranking Viking women have uncovered the remains of fine clothing, housewares, and jewelry. Some graves also contain the skeletons of slaves sacrificed to serve their mistress in the next world.

Chapter III

FARMERS AND SETTLERS

The great majority of Vikings were farmers. They belonged to the social class known as freemen. This large and varied group also included merchants, artisans, and all other free working people.

The lowest-ranking farmers were landless peasants who hired themselves out as servants or laborers. Tenant farmers rented plots of land from wealthy landowners, paying with a portion of their harvest. The most respected farmers owned and worked their own farms, which ranged from small plots to large estates.

Despite their differences in wealth and status, all freemen shared certain rights and privileges. These included protection under the law, the right to bear arms, and the right to take part in the democratic assemblies called **Things.**

In the Longhouse

The Scandinavian farmer's way of life was shaped by the land. In Norway, where the soil was thin and rocky, most people lived on isolated farms. In Denmark and parts of Sweden, there were large areas of fertile land. There groups of farms often clustered together in small villages.

Most of what we know about farm life comes from excavations of Danish farming villages. Digging through the layers of earth that cover old settlements, archaeologists have found traces of plants, animal bones, tools, household goods, and buildings.

The main building on a Viking farm was the **longhouse.** This long rectangular dwelling might be built from wood, **turf,** or **wattle and daub.** A wattle-and-daub house was made by weaving

The Viking longhouse was a simple structure built more for warmth than for beauty. This reconstructed longhouse can help us understand how farm families lived.

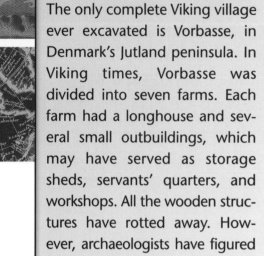

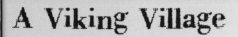

A Viking Village

The only complete Viking village ever excavated is Vorbasse, in Denmark's Jutland peninsula. In Viking times, Vorbasse was divided into seven farms. Each farm had a longhouse and several small outbuildings, which may have served as storage sheds, servants' quarters, and workshops. All the wooden structures have rotted away. However, archaeologists have figured out their basic design from dark marks left in the light-colored soil. They know that the longhouses contained many large animal stalls. That tells us that the farmers' main business was probably cattle raising. Excavators have also found many fragments of fine imported pottery and lava millstones. These show that Vorbasse was a prosperous village, with extra produce to trade for goods from far-off lands.

together twigs and branches (the "wattle") and plastering them with a "daub" of mud or clay.

Wooden partitions divided the longhouse into two or three sections. The main room served as the living quarters. One end of the house was a barn, with stalls for the cattle and other livestock. There also might be a small kitchen, grain barn, or dairy.

In the center of the house was a hearth for heat, light, and cooking. Smoke from the fire hung in the air or escaped through a hole in the roof. Benches lined the walls, serving as seats by day and beds by night. There might be a chair for the head of the household. Often the only other furnishings were stools, a weaving loom, a board for meals, and wooden storage chests.

This warm, smoky, noisy, crowded hall was home to the farm family and their servants and slaves. Here the Vikings ate, slept, worked, played, and gathered around the fire to tell tales of gods and heroes.

A Family Affair

The farm family was a large, close-knit group. It often included not only a couple and their children but also the farmer's parents and unmarried brothers and sisters. To the Vikings, these family ties were sacred. The members of a family owed one another loyalty and support. They were expected to care for their aged and disabled relatives. They also had a duty to defend the family honor by avenging insulted or injured kinsmen. That sacred obligation could turn a dispute between two men into a bloody feud involving dozens of people from both families.

A glimpse of the farmer's busy life comes from the poem *Rigsthula*. Karl, the mythical ancestor of all farmers, is described as a strong man who "tamed the oxen and **tempered** ploughshares, timbered houses and barns for the hay, fashioned carts, and followed the plow." Along with their wooden plows, farmers used wooden shovels and iron-bladed hoes and digging sticks to work the soil. They planted grains and vegetables suited to the harsh northern climate, such as barley, oats, rye, wheat, peas, and cabbage. To harvest their crops, they used iron **sickles,** sharp **scythes,** and special broad-bladed cutting tools known as **leaf-knives.**

All farmers raised at least a few animals. Their livestock might include cattle, sheep, pigs, and sometimes goats, hens, geese, and ducks. In some areas, animal farming was more important than raising crops. Many farmers also fished, trapped, and hunted.

In their spare hours, farmers worked in the longhouse or workshop, crafting everything from tools and weapons to lamps and

A modern woman dressed in traditional Scandinavian clothing practices Viking-style weaving.

cooking pots. Nearly everything the family needed was made at home, so the men and women of the farm had to be skilled in many different crafts.

Women's Work

While the men of the household spent most of their time outdoors, the women worked in the longhouse. One of their most important jobs was preparing the family's meals. That time-consuming task included a host of chores. Farm women had to milk the cows, collect the eggs, churn butter, make cheese, grind grain, bake bread, brew ale and mead, mix porridge, and roast, bake, or boil fish and meat.

Women also spent many hours spinning, weaving, and dyeing wool and linen, then cutting and sewing the family's clothes. They supervised the servants and slaves. They cared for the children. All but the youngest farm children had chores. Sons helped their fathers in the fields and workshops, while daughters worked beside their mothers in the longhouse.

Although their lives were mostly limited to the home, Viking farmwives enjoyed a higher status than women in many other parts of the world. A wife had the right to own and inherit property. If her marriage was unsuccessful, she could get a divorce. When her husband was away from home, she had full responsibility for the farm and household.

These keys may have belonged to a Viking farmwife.

The farmwife wore a bunch of keys on a belt at her waist. The keys secured the farm buildings and the wooden chests that held the family's most valued possessions. They were also a symbol of the farmwife's respected status and authority.

Away from Home

Once or twice a year, a farmer left home to attend a meeting of the Thing. All free adult men had the right to attend their local assembly, where issues concerning the community were decided. Larger regional assemblies were attended by representatives chosen from the local Thing. These meetings handled wide-ranging issues such as approving new laws proposed by the king.

Things met outdoors, often on a hilltop or low earth platform. The proceedings were loud, lively, and long. Members might propose changes in local laws regarding trade, marriage, or some other aspect of society. After a long debate, the assembly would reach a decision. Members would show their approval by shouting and rattling their weapons. Laws were memorized and handed down orally.

Assemblies also served as courts of law. When a man brought a complaint against a neighbor, a jury was chosen to hear witnesses and pronounce judgment. The penalty for crime was usually a fine, which was paid to the victim or the victim's family. Fines varied according to the victim's status. A Viking found guilty of killing a jarl paid a higher fine than the murderer of an ordinary freeman. There were no police to enforce judgments. It was up to the victim's family to make sure the sentence was carried out.

A convicted man who refused to accept the judgment of the Thing could be outlawed. That meant he was placed outside the protection of the law. Outlaws usually went into exile, since anyone could harm them without fear of punishment.

Besides their legal duties, freemen sometimes had other reasons for venturing away from home. In the summer months, when his workload lightened, a farmer might go trading. Loading his boat or wagon with extra produce or homespun linen, he traveled to the nearest trading town. There he could swap his goods for items that were unavailable at home, such as iron bars or imported pottery.

Another kind of venture offered more risks as well as the chance of greater rewards. A farmer who was ambitious and adventurous could join a raiding party. Many able young freemen

Many Viking men made their fortunes by joining raiding parties and traveling by ship to far lands.

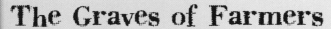

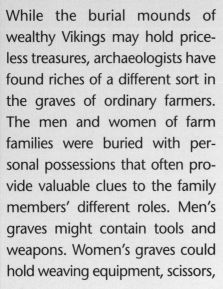

The Graves of Farmers

While the burial mounds of wealthy Vikings may hold priceless treasures, archaeologists have found riches of a different sort in the graves of ordinary farmers. The men and women of farm families were buried with personal possessions that often provide valuable clues to the family members' different roles. Men's graves might contain tools and weapons. Women's graves could hold weaving equipment, scissors, needles, and cooking utensils. Personal items show that Viking women took pride in their appearance. Archaeologists have dug up hair combs, tweezers, and pairs of bronze oval brooches, which were used to fasten the straps of a woman's gown. Some graves contain jewelry from foreign lands. These prized possessions may have been plunder brought home by a part-time raider for his wife or girlfriend.

built their fortunes on foreign expeditions, fighting with the warrior bands of successful chieftains.

North Atlantic Pioneers

The greatest problem Scandinavian farmers faced was the shortage of good land. "Land hunger" prompted some hardy settlers to venture west, into the uncharted waters of the North Atlantic Ocean.

Around the year 860, sailors who were blown off course on a voyage from Sweden became the first Vikings to reach Iceland. According to the twelfth-century *Book of Icelanders,* these accidental explorers found a vast land "covered with forest between mountain and seashore." Settlers soon arrived to claim their share of the riches. By 930, there were some 30,000 Vikings living in

Erik the Red's son Leif Eriksson carried on his father's tradition of exploration and discovery. This dramatic illustration celebrates Leif's voyage from Greenland to North America.

thriving settlements along Iceland's coasts and in the fertile river valleys. They brought their traditions with them. Icelanders built turf longhouses modeled on Norwegian farmhouses. They made most of their own tools, weapons, household articles, and clothing. Iceland was governed by the Althing, an assembly of freemen that met for two weeks every summer.

L'Anse aux Meadows

Around the year 1000, the Viking explorer Leif Eriksson founded a short-lived colony in North America, which he named Vinland. In 1961, Norwegian explorer Helge Ingstad and his wife, archaeologist Anne Stine, set out to find that historic site. Following old maps and clues from the sagas, they retraced Leif's travels. Their search led to the remains of an old settlement in L'Anse aux Meadows, a village in northern Newfoundland. There the Ingstads uncovered the foundations of long turf houses built around 1000. They also found an Icelandic stone lamp and a bronze pin for fastening a Viking man's cloak. Not all scholars agree that L'Anse aux Meadows was really the site of Leif Eriksson's Vinland. However, the settlement does prove that venturesome Vikings reached North America nearly five hundred years before Columbus.

Historians have reconstructed the Viking Age settlement discovered at L'Anse aux Meadows.

Around 983, a hot-tempered Icelander named Erik the Red was outlawed for killing two neighbors in a feud. Erik sailed west in search of a safe place to spend his exile. He came to an immense land half covered in ice and snow, inhabited by a small population of Eskimos. Erik named the island Greenland, hoping that "men would be drawn to go there if the land had an attractive name." In time his new colony would attract some three thousand Viking settlers.

Erik's son Leif inherited his father's pioneering spirit. Around the year 1000, Leif Eriksson set out from Greenland, seeking new lands even farther to the west. According to the thirteenth-century *Erik's Saga,* Leif "ran into prolonged difficulties at sea, and finally came upon lands whose existence he had never suspected. There were fields of wild wheat growing there, and vines."

Landing on the shores of "Vinland," Leif and his men became the first Europeans to set foot in North America. They spent the winter there, but no permanent Viking settlement was ever built. Today, historians are still debating the exact location of Leif Eriksson's Vinland.

Viking artisans made beautiful items, such as this brooch.

Chapter IV

ARTISANS AND ARTISTS

The early Scandinavians were remarkable artisans, or craftspeople. Many crafts were practiced in the home, where farm families produced a variety of practical and beautiful objects.

Around the beginning of the Viking Age, some freemen began to specialize in specific crafts. Many of these skilled artisans lived and worked in large trading centers in Scandinavia and abroad. Some were employed in the households of kings and other rich and powerful people. Some traveled from place to place, selling their goods and services wherever they found a demand. While most artisans were men, historians believe that women also worked in crafts, either alone or as partners in the family business.

Viking artisans embellished nearly everything they made with complex, imaginative designs. Their decorations turned even commonplace objects into works of art. In fact, the Vikings had no separate word for "artist." The skilled craftspeople who created everything from combs to woven tapestries to intricately carved wooden ships were all known as *smidr,* or "smiths."

This wood carving shows a Viking craftsman hammering heated iron to make a sword.

A Variety of Styles

Most of what we know about Viking arts and crafts has come from archaeological finds. Historians have learned how artisans worked by studying the remains of workshops and objects found in both humble graves and rich burial mounds.

Archaeologists often use artistic styles to date their finds. Most Viking art featured designs of real and imaginary animals. The way smiths portrayed these creatures changed over time. By

A Lost Toolbox

In 1936, a farmer on the Swedish island of Gotland made a remarkable discovery. While plowing a field, he came across an old iron chain. Digging deeper, he found that the chain was wrapped around a large oak chest. Inside the box were more than two hundred objects. There were blacksmith and carpenter tools, iron bars, and half-finished projects including locks, keys, and bells. Archaeologists dated the find to around the year 1000. At that time, the field was a soggy bog. The toolbox may have belonged to a traveling smith who lost it while crossing the waters. His accident turned into a lucky find for historians, providing valuable information on the variety of tools and techniques used by Viking craftsmen.

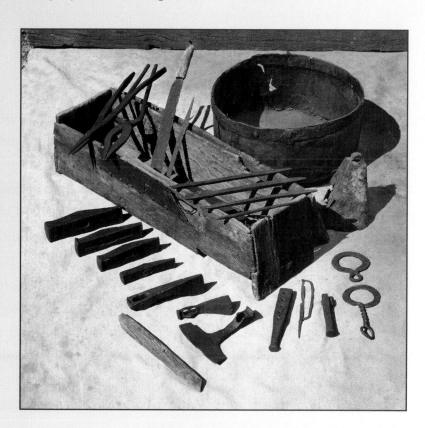

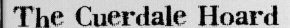

The Cuerdale Hoard

Sometimes archaeologists are able to date artifacts from the inscriptions on coins found along with the other treasures. Before wealthy Vikings went on a journey, they often buried their most valuable possessions for safekeeping. More than a thousand of these treasure hoards have been discovered, centuries after being hidden by owners who never returned to dig up their riches. The largest hoard was unearthed in 1840 by workmen repairing a river embankment near Cuerdale, England. The Cuerdale hoard contained 88 pounds (40 kilograms) of silver, including coins, brooches, arm rings, neck rings, combs, bars, and buckles. The inscriptions on the coins revealed that this massive treasure was buried around 910.

studying a wide variety of artifacts, historians have created a "calendar" of Scandinavian art styles from different time periods.

Most of the Scandinavian styles were named after the place where a famous example of objects decorated in that style was found. For example, the earliest art style is called Oseberg. Its name came from the famous ninth-century ship burial discovered at Oseberg farm in Norway. (The Oseberg ship burial is described on page 30.) The treasures in this burial mound were covered with a multitude of "gripping beasts." These strange, slithery creatures look like a combination of bears, lions, dogs, and other animals, with sharp claws that grasp everything within reach. When archaeologists discover an object with similar designs, they know that it was created around the same time as the Oseberg treasures.

A close-up photograph shows an animal head carving from a sledge found with the Oseberg ship.

Honored Smiths

Viking artisans worked in many different materials. Sculptors inscribed stones with pictures and messages. Leatherworkers tanned animal hides to make shoes and boots. Weavers wove wool and linen, which were used for everyday clothing and fine decorative tapestries. Wood carvers decorated cups, wagons, warships, and many other objects with elaborate designs. Other skilled carvers crafted items such as combs, spoons, and game pieces from animal bones and horns, deer antlers, and walrus tusks.

Both men and women admired the jeweler's art. Archaeologists excavating the workshops of Viking jewelers have found thousands of clay molds used to produce women's bronze oval brooches. Jewelers also made colorful glass beads and highly prized **amber** beads, charms, and pendants.

The most valuable jewelry was made from silver and gold. Only the wealthiest Vikings could afford the intricately decorated necklaces, bracelets, pendants, and brooches handcrafted by expert silversmiths and goldsmiths. Rich people also showed off their wealth by wearing plain but costly arm and neck rings. Arab traveler Ibn Fadlan, who met Viking merchants in Russia in the 920s, observed that the women wore "neck rings of gold and silver, one for each 10,000 dirhems [Arab currency] which her husband is worth; some women have many."

The most respected of all artisans were the blacksmiths. These skilled craftsmen shaped iron into essential objects such as farm tools, cooking pots, and nails and rivets for shipbuilding. Weaponsmiths welded together different types of iron to create high-quality spears, axes, and swords. The best swords were strong, sharp, and flexible. Their hilts were decorated with intricate designs in bronze or precious metals. A fine sword might

At the Lofotr Viking Museum in Norway, visitors can experience the sights and sounds of a recreated Viking blacksmith shop.

even have its own name, such as Golden-hilt, Long-and-sharp, or Leg-biter.

Skilled weaponsmiths often worked for a king or chieftain, making weapons for the ruler and his warriors. Viking legends confirm the high standing of these honored artisans. In one old tale, a master smith named Regin forges a mighty sword that has the power to slay a magical dragon.

Ships and Shipbuilders

Another highly respected group of artisans were the shipbuilders. There were two main types of Viking ships. Longships carried warriors into battle. Trade ships took merchants and their cargo to trading centers and transported explorers and settlers to distant lands.

All Viking ships had the same basic design. The master shipbuilder and his crew of skilled carpenters used axes and wedges to split logs into thin, flexible planks. They built up the ship's hull by overlapping the planks and fastening them with iron rivets. Both ends of the ship curved up to a point, which might be carved with the figure of a dragon or other powerful beast. There was a single mast and a wide rectangular sail. Ships were steered by a right-side **rudder**. This "steering board" gave us our modern word for the right side of a ship, "starboard."

Longships were long, low, and narrow and were designed to ride swiftly in both deep and shallow waters. They could be powered by either oars or sails. A Christian monk who watched Danish king Svein Forkbeard's fleet set sail was awed by the "towered ships . . . painted with ornate colours [and] covered with gold and silver figures." The monk described glittering images of dolphins, lions, fire-breathing dragons, and "bulls with necks raised high."

Trade ships were shorter and broader than warships. Cargo

Modern Viking Voyages

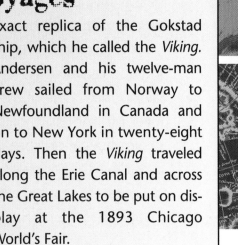

Modern-day historians and adventurers have built dozens of Viking ships modeled after archaeological finds. One of the first was a reproduction of the Gokstad ship. This tenth-century longship was discovered in a burial mound in Vestfold, Norway, in 1880. A few years later, Norwegian seafarer Magnus Andersen set sail in a nearly exact replica of the Gokstad ship, which he called the *Viking.* Andersen and his twelve-man crew sailed from Norway to Newfoundland in Canada and on to New York in twenty-eight days. Then the *Viking* traveled along the Erie Canal and across the Great Lakes to be put on display at the 1893 Chicago World's Fair.

Viking shipbuilders use axes and other tools to build a sturdy wooden vessel.

and livestock were carried in an open hold. These sturdy vessels had a few oars for maneuvering in tight spots, but they were mainly propelled by sails.

Archaeologists have excavated many sites used for shipbuilding and repair. They have also studied the ships discovered in burial mounds. One of their most exciting finds came from a narrow inlet off the port of Roskilde, Denmark. In the 1950s, divers exploring the bottom of the channel discovered five Viking ships, including the longest longship ever found. The vessels had been deliberately sunk sometime around the year 1000 to prevent invaders from entering the waterway.

MERCHANTS AND TRADERS

A century before the first raiders went a-viking, Scandinavian merchants were traveling to trading centers along the coasts of western Europe. It was their reports of rich, unguarded monasteries and port cities that launched the Viking Age.

Trade flourished in Viking times. Merchant ships loaded with valuable cargo sailed along an extensive trading network that stretched all the way from Greenland to central Asia. At the same time, foreign merchants from many lands came to Scandinavia's busy market towns.

Some visitors recorded their observations. English traders in the Danish town of Hedeby wrote that the townsmen combed their hair and bathed every Saturday, which made them very attractive to the ladies. Arab traveler Ibrahim al-Tartushi was less complimentary. He described Hedeby as "an appalling place" where heathens honored their gods by sacrificing animals and hanging the carcasses on poles outside their houses. Even more unpleasant, he wrote, was the "dreadful singing of these people, worse even than the barking of dogs."

Busy Trading Towns

The first Scandinavian towns developed during the Viking Age. In earlier times, farmers, artisans, and merchants had gathered for a

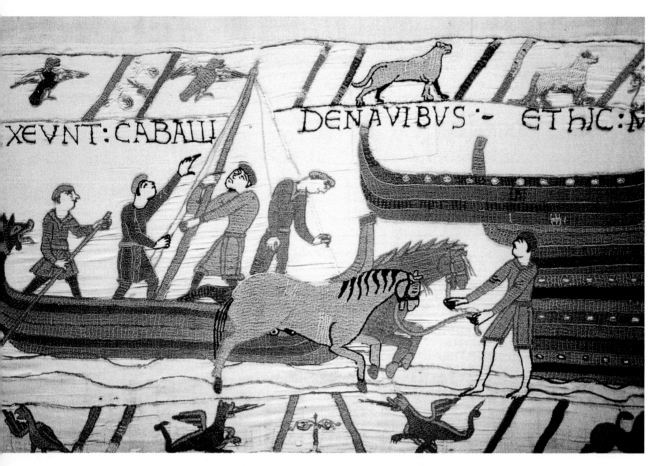

XEVNT:CABALL DENAVIBVS ETHIC:

A tapestry from the 1000s shows a crew of Norman men arriving in England by ship. The Vikings conducted trade with people from nearly every part of the known world.

few weeks each year to buy and sell goods at seasonal market centers. The Viking kings wanted a way to profit from those exchanges. They founded permanent trading settlements on sheltered harbors and inland waterways connected to the sea. As the towns prospered, the royal treasuries swelled with taxes and tolls paid by merchants and travelers.

A Viking town was a noisy, crowded place. The bustle began at the waterfront. There workers labored on small boats and large merchant ships, loading and unloading cargo. Stretching away from the waterfront were narrow streets paved with wooden planks. The walkways were lined with small rectangular houses built of wood or wattle and daub. Sprinkled among the houses were vendors' stalls and tents pitched by visiting traders. There were also many workshops. Excavations of Viking trading centers have uncovered shops where artisans made products from iron, bone, antler, wood, leather, silver, bronze, amber, and glass.

The merchants in Viking towns bought and sold a wide variety of goods. On display in their stores or stalls were foods, furs, cloth, and walrus tusks brought to town by Scandinavian farmers and hunters. More exotic items came from Viking raiding and trading expeditions and from the cargoes of foreign trade vessels. Archaeologists excavating the graves of rich merchants in the Swedish town of Birka have found artifacts from all over the world. These include swords from Frankia, dyed wool from Frisia, glass and pottery from the Rhineland of western Germany, brocades from the Byzantine Empire, leather belts from Persia, and silk from China.

Viking merchants and settlers also established trading centers overseas. They founded the first towns in Ireland, including the present-day capital, Dublin. In England, the Viking town of Jorvik was one of Europe's largest and most prosperous cities.

Historians have rebuilt the Viking trading town of Hedeby, in what was once Denmark but is now part of Germany. This photograph shows a log street believed to have been built in Viking times.

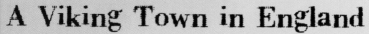

A Viking Town in England

In 866, Danish warriors captured a trading center on the site of present-day York, England. Within a few years, the small town they called Jorvik had grown into the capital of the Danelaw, a Viking kingdom that would control most of northern England for almost a century.

In the 1970s, archaeologists began extensive excavations at York. Over the years, they uncovered the remains of tenth-century houses and workshops, along with hundreds of thousands of artifacts. Some finds related to crafts and trade. These included merchants' scales, artisans' tools, and iron dies for making coins. Other artifacts painted a picture of everyday life. Among these were wool socks, leather shoes, dice, board games, and ice skates. The excavators also dug up a set of wooden panpipes that could still play simple musical tunes.

Silver and Coins

Early Viking merchants did not buy and sell goods with money. Instead, they exchanged merchandise by **bartering.** A farmer with a load of fox furs might want millstones for grinding grain and bronze brooches for his wife. A foreign trader bearing jars of white wine from the Rhineland might have a craving for furs, ivory, or amber. Buyer and seller would haggle over the exchange and strike a deal.

Buyers also might pay with foreign coins. To a Viking trader, the value assigned to a coin didn't matter, only its weight in silver. Every merchant carried a set of scales, which were used for weighing silver by balancing it against small chunks of iron. To make amounts come out even, the merchant might toss in small pieces of silver hacked from coins or jewelry. Viking treasure hoards often contain **hacksilver** along with other valuables.

In the ninth century, the Vikings began to mint their own coins. The first Scandinavian coins were imitations of foreign money. Later, kings began to issue coins stamped with their names and titles. Some coins reflected the Vikings' gradual conversion from paganism to Christianity. One penny minted in Jorvik carried the name of Saint Peter alongside a hammer, the symbol of the pagan god Thor.

Trading Expeditions

While some merchants in large market towns made their living entirely from trade, most Viking traders were part-timers. In the warm summer months, farmers, hunters, and artisans might seek their fortunes on trading expeditions. Sometimes they traveled as part of a **félag,** or "fellowship," with each member receiving an equal share of the profits.

There was a fine line between trading and raiding. One saga describes the adventures of a Viking named Thorolf, who sailed to Finland with "plenty of wares for trading." Meeting a band of less well-armed Finns, Thorolf and his men "took of them the tribute, and held a fair with them. All was managed with goodwill and friendship, though not without fear on the Finns' side." Later, the travelers came across another company of merchant-warriors. They "slew near upon a hundred, and took immense booty [plunder]."

Viking trade ships were built to carry heavy loads of cargo. Ships leaving Scandinavia might be crammed with furs, walrus tusks, sealskins, **soapstone,** amber, dried fish, and slaves. Traders

A Viking trader would have used scales like these to weigh silver and other valuables.

This bronze statue of the Buddha, discovered on the Swedish island of Helgö, was made in India in the 400s.

Ibn Fadlan and the Rus

In 922, Arab traveler Ibn Fadlan met Viking traders in what is now Russia. "I have never seen more perfect physical specimens, tall as date palms, blonde and ruddy," he wrote. "Each man has an axe, a sword, and a knife and keeps each by him at all times."

At the start of a trading expedition, wrote Ibn Fadlan, the Rus laid offerings of food and drink before wooden idols. They asked the gods to send a wealthy merchant "who will buy from me whatever I wish." Later, they returned and thanked the gods with animal sacrifices. "In the night, dogs come and eat all," noted the skeptical writer, "but the one who has made the offering says, 'Truly, my Lord is content with me and has consumed the present I brought him.' "

generally returned from their voyages with luxury items, including silver, swords, wine, pottery, glass, and spices.

Exotic objects sometimes traveled vast distances as they were passed along from one trader to another. In 1950, archaeologists on the Swedish island of Helgö dug up a bronze figure of the Buddha. Crafted more than 5,000 miles (8,000 kilometers) away in northern India, the elegant statue had somehow found its way to a Viking marketplace.

The Vikings in Russia

Most Vikings traded over short distances, traveling to and from ports along the Scandinavian and Baltic coasts. There were also frequent expeditions to the colonies in Iceland and Greenland and to the Viking kingdoms in England, Ireland, and France. A

An illustration depicts the arrival of Viking adventurers in what is now Russia.

few adventurous traders journeyed all the way to Constantinople (modern-day Istanbul), Baghdad, and the shores of North Africa.

In the eighth century, Swedish warrior-merchants blazed a trail into eastern Europe. Crossing the Baltic Sea, they hauled their ships overland to two great rivers, the Dnieper and the Volga. The daring travelers followed the dangerous river waters southward, past rocks, rapids, and waterfalls, to reach the land of the Slavs. There they founded a kingdom based on trading cities including Novgorod and Kiev. The Slavs called the invaders "Rus." Over the centuries, the Rus state expanded, and the area they settled became known as Russia.

Chapter VI

WARRIORS

Every free Viking man carried a weapon. There was no telling when he might have to fight to defend his land, property, or honor. One popular poem cautioned that a man "should not walk unarmed, but have his weapons to hand. He knows not when he may need a spear, or what menace meet on the road."

Freemen also needed their weapons to join raiding expeditions and to defend the kingdom in times of war. For a Viking, warfare was the most honored of all activities. Poems and sagas celebrated the daring, deadly warriors who followed their king or chieftain into battle. "I've been with sword and spear slippery with bright blood," proclaimed the proud hero of Snorri Sturluson's *Egil's Saga.* "And how well we violent Vikings clashed! Red flames ate up men's roofs, raging we killed and killed."

Hit-and-Run Armies

All able-bodied freemen had a duty to answer the king's call to defend their country. Under some rulers, the Scandinavian kingdoms were divided into units, each with a certain number of farms. When danger threatened, the king could call on the units to contribute their share of fighting men, ships, or supplies.

While ordinary farmers might go to war in times of trouble, the backbone of the Viking armies were the warrior bands. The band of loyal warriors sworn into the service of a ruler was called a ***lid***. A local chieftain's lid might be large enough to man a

This memorial stone is decorated with images of Viking warriors and a longship. When the stone was first carved, the images would have been highlighted with brightly colored paint.

longship. A king's lid could include enough troops for an entire fleet. The armies that raided the monasteries of western Europe at the start of the Viking Age were made up of groups of lid, gathered together to achieve a common goal.

In later times, some warriors became **mercenaries.** These professional soldiers fought solely for pay. When Svein Forkbeard invaded England in 1013, his army included many lid plus a large force of mercenaries.

Women as Warriors

The Icelandic sagas contain tales of strong-willed women who used their wits, and occasionally their swords, to get their way. In 1200, the Danish historian Saxo Grammaticus backed up that claim. "There were once women in Denmark," he wrote, "who dressed themselves to look like men [and] sought the clash of arms rather than the arm's embrace."

Historians have never found any reliable evidence that Viking women really took part in warfare. However, they do know that warriors sometimes brought their wives with them on foreign campaigns. According to the *Anglo-Saxon Chronicle,* wives and children traveled with the Vikings who invaded England in the ninth century. The women performed valuable services for the army, cooking, mending clothes, and caring for the sick and injured.

Even the largest Viking armies probably numbered just a few thousand men. Their success depended not on superior size or strategy but on surprise. Warriors in swift longships could swoop down on settlements along the seacoasts and shallow inland waterways. By the time the defenders assembled their forces, the attackers were already on their way back to sea with their prizes. One Irish scholar described the hit-and-run Viking forces as a "rushing North Wind."

Dressed to Kill

The sagas and European chronicles portrayed the Vikings as fearsome fighters skilled in the use of a variety of weapons. The pagan custom of burying men with their prized possessions has helped historians learn about the weapons these warriors wielded.

A warrior's most prized weapon was his sword. Archaeologists have discovered thousands of strong iron swords crafted in dozens of different styles. Most Viking swords were double edged. Unlike a slender sword with a sharp, stabbing point, a double-edged sword was used for hacking at the enemy.

Another common weapon was the spear. There were light-weight spears for throwing and heavier ones for stabbing in close fighting. According to the sagas, skilled spearsmen could throw two spears at once. Some could even turn an enemy's spear against him after catching it in midflight.

Many warriors carried battle-axes. Light axes were held in one hand, while heavy double-headed broadaxes were wielded with two hands. Other weapons frequently found in Viking graves include long fighting knives and bows and arrows.

Warriors protected themselves with round wooden shields, often covered with leather and painted in bright colors. They

Double-edged swords such as the two shown here were the favorite weapons of most Viking warriors.

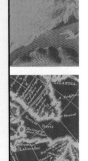

Hornless Helmets

The two-horned helmets worn by Vikings in paintings and movies are a myth. Most warriors protected their heads with bowl-shaped leather caps. Chieftains may have owned more deluxe headgear. Carved stones on the Swedish island of Gotland show war leaders wearing cone-shaped helmets, perhaps made of iron.

The only complete Viking helmet ever found came from a tenth-century grave in southern Norway. It had a gogglelike visor and chain mail hanging down the back to protect the neck. The helmet must have belonged to a rich and powerful chieftain. His grave also held fragments of an expensive chain-mail tunic and a splendid sword inlaid with copper and silver designs.

wore little armor. Most fighters had a hardened leather cap and a leather tunic, sometimes reinforced with bone plates. A few leaders owned chain-mail shirts. Chain mail was made from thousands of small iron rings, which were forged separately and then linked with rivets. That long, difficult production process made mail armor too expensive for all but the wealthiest warlords.

Battle Stations!

Despite their fierce reputation, the Vikings' main strategy in warfare seems to have been to *avoid* battle whenever possible. An invading army fighting a pitched battle on enemy soil was almost always outnumbered. Raiders preferred to strike unexpectedly and escape quickly with their plunder.

When battle was unavoidable, the Vikings usually fought on foot. Troops were not organized in strict military formations.

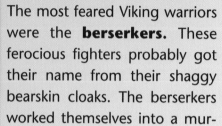

Going Berserk

The most feared Viking warriors were the **berserkers.** These ferocious fighters probably got their name from their shaggy bearskin cloaks. The berserkers worked themselves into a mur- derous rage before battle. They howled, bit their shields, and fought wildly, heedless of danger and pain. Their crazed behavior gave us the English word "berserk."

Instead, each man fought in a group with his leader and comrades. Often, the younger warriors lined up in front, overlapping their shields to form a defensive "shield wall." Older veterans assembled behind them in support. A bodyguard of handpicked warriors formed around each chieftain. The king fought at the head of the army. Marking his place in the field was his banner, carried by an honored warrior known as the standard bearer.

Before the battle, the king would make a rousing speech. The warriors tried to intimidate their opponents with wild battle cries. A single spear hurled over enemy lines signaled the start of combat. Next came a shower of spears and arrows. An old English poem about a battle between Viking invaders and the English army recalled "the loud clamor" raised by the "wolves of slaughter. . . . Then they sent forth from their hands shafts hard as file, murderously sharpened spears flew. Bows were busily at work."

Finally, the armies would charge, meeting in fierce hand-to-hand combat. A commander might lead a group of warriors in a wedge-shaped formation to try to break through the enemy's shield wall. Success was assured when the wall was broken and the leader's banner fell.

**The bold adventurer Erik the Red defeats an enemy in hand-to-hand combat.
Viking leaders always fought at the head of their armies.**

A Warriors' Paradise

Written sources mention only a few Viking sea battles. Most of these encounters pitted one group of Scandinavian seamen against another. The defenders usually lashed their longships together to form a fighting platform. The attackers fired arrows and tossed grappling lines, trying to board the enemy's ships. If they succeeded, they went to work clearing the decks with their swords, spears, and axes. Often the conflict ended with the loyal warriors of the losing fleet gathering around their leader, joining him in a glorious last stand.

The courage of Viking warriors was inspired not only by dreams of glory and honor but also by their belief in **Valhalla.** This paradise was the home of the pagan god Odin. The souls of men who died bravely in battle were led to Valhalla by maiden warriors called **Valkyries.**

In Odin's golden hall, heroic warriors enjoyed a daily round of feasts and combat. The battles helped them perfect their fighting skills, in preparation for **Ragnarök,** or "Doom of the Gods." Ragnarök would bring the world to an end, in a final battle pitting evil beasts and giants against the gods and their chosen warriors. After the destruction, a new earth would rise from the sea, and a new race of gods and men would "abide in joy and serenity during long ages."

The Valkyries were mythical women warriors who were believed to live in Valhalla, the great hall of the high god Odin. According to Norse myths and legends, the souls of brave warriors who died in battle were carried to Valhalla by the Valkyries.

Chapter VII

POETS AND RUNE MASTERS

The Vikings had no books. However, that does not mean that they were illiterate. Sometime around the first century A.D., the Scandinavian people began to write with letters called **runes.** Runic inscriptions on memorial stones and other objects are a valuable source of information on the Viking world because they are the only writing left by the Vikings themselves.

The Vikings also had a strong tradition of oral literature. They passed down stories from generation to generation by word of mouth. Most of their literature was in the form of poetry. After the Viking Age, many of the early poems were preserved in the sagas and other Icelandic writings.

Writing in Runes

Ancient peoples in many parts of western Europe wrote in runes. As they converted to Christianity, these different groups gradually switched to the Roman alphabet of the Church. Because the Scandinavians adopted Christianity later than other Europeans, they kept their runic writing long after it had disappeared everywhere else.

Magic Words

The Vikings believed that runes had magical properties. Carving the right words on a sword could ensure the owner victory in battle. Runes written on a pregnant woman's palms could help her safely deliver her child. It took great knowledge and skill to work rune magic. One Viking poet cautioned, "Let no man carve runes to cast a spell, save [unless] first he learns to read them well."

The rune carvers weren't the only people credited with special powers. The sagas contain many tales of men and women who used magic to tell fortunes, find lost objects, or bring rain to crops. One woman in Greenland "carried a staff with a knob on the end and on her belt . . . hung a charm pouch." Traveling from farm to farm, this fortune teller used her magic charms and songs to contact the spirits and ask them questions about the farmers' destinies.

The runic alphabet was called **futhark,** after the sounds of its first six letters. In Viking times, the futhark had sixteen runes. These characters were formed from straight lines instead of curves, in order to make them easier to carve in wood, bone, metal, or stone. Carving still takes more time and effort than writing with a pen or brush, so most inscriptions were fairly short.

The Vikings used runes to send brief messages carved on twigs. They also inscribed their names on storage chests, brooches, weapons, and other prized possessions. A bone comb case found in a Viking settlement in England boasts, "Thorfast made a good comb." A silver neck ring from a treasure hoard in Norway reads, "We paid a visit to the lads of Frisia and we it was who split the spoils of battle."

No one knows how many Vikings could read and write. However, archaeologists have found thousands of objects scratched with their owner's mark, which makes them believe that most people knew at least a few words.

It is believed that women as well as men could be literate. A wooden weaving tablet found in Lund, Sweden, bears the curious phrase, "Sigvor's Ingemar shall have my weeping—*aallatti!*" Some scholars interpret this as a message written by a Viking woman whose lover (Ingemar) had rejected her for a rival. The angry woman scratched her inscription in the wood, then added the final magic word to trigger her curse.

Stones of Remembrance

The most common Viking inscriptions are found on rune stones. Hundreds of these messages can still be read on cliff faces and boulders in Scandinavia and abroad. Rune stones were usually inscribed by a professional rune master. These skilled carvers often signed their work. Archaeologists have found more than eighty inscriptions carved by one eleventh-century Swedish rune master named Opir.

Most rune stones were raised in memory of the dead. Memorial stones usually bore a simple inscription honoring a father or mother, husband or wife, loyal follower or valued trading partner. A typical stone in Sweden reads, "Thorkunn and Bruni had this monument made, in memory of their father Igulfast."

More elaborate memorials might give details of a loved one's life and death, including the names of relatives and a summary of landholdings. Historians believe that these stones had a double purpose. They not only honored the dead but also served as a public notice establishing the right of the heirs to inherit property.

Some rune stones were inscribed with poetry and elaborate

This rune stone was raised on the Swedish island of Öland in the 900s. It honors the memory of a Danish chieftain named Sibbe the Good, who may have come to the island to wage war.

designs. One memorial in southern Sweden is covered with runes carved inside the image of a long twisting snake. The inscription pays tribute to a young adventurer who died on an expedition to the east.

> Tola had this stone put up in memory of her son Harald,
>   Ingvar's brother:
> Like men they traveled far for gold
> And in the east they fed the eagle [killed their enemies],
> In the south they died.

The Jelling Stones

The most famous rune stones are at Jelling, on Denmark's Jutland peninsula. In the mid-tenth century, King Gorm erected a memorial stone at Jelling, inscribed in memory of Thorvi, his queen. Beside the boulder was a pagan monument, a group of stones arranged in the outline of a ship.

When Gorm's son Harald Bluetooth converted to Christianity, he destroyed the "stone ship" setting. Harald moved his father's body from its pagan burial mound to a grave beneath a wooden church. He also erected a huge memorial stone decorated with spectacular carvings, including an image of Christ. The inscription on the stone boasts, "It was this Harald who won for himself all Denmark and Norway and made the Danes Christians."

One side of the rune stone erected by Harald Bluetooth at Jelling is decorated with an image of Christ, with his arms spread out and a halo above his head.

Honored Skalds

The best-known poetry of the Viking Age was composed by skalds. These professional poets enjoyed a prestigious place in Viking society. Skalds lived in the households of chieftains or kings, or they traveled from court to court. They entertained the audiences at feasts and other public gatherings by chanting or singing their verses. Most of the skalds' works were praise poems, describing the generosity, heroic exploits, and remarkable achievements of the poet's host. Skalds also composed funeral poems, ensuring a ruler's lasting fame.

Skaldic poetry was composed in several different forms. All of them were extremely complicated. The poet had to arrange the words in a strict number of syllables, with internal rhymes and alliteration (beginning words with the same sound) at specific points. Skaldic verse also made elaborate use of **kennings,** or fanciful metaphors for common words. A kenning for "ship" might be "wave's horse" or "steed of the sea." A sword might be called an "icicle of war" or the "fire of Odin."

The strict patterns and rhymes of skaldic poetry were designed to help poets remember their verses. Popular poems were recited over and over, down through the generations. In the late twelfth century, when the Scandinavians began to write down their history, they used the old poems as sources. The writers of the Icelandic sagas sprinkled skaldic verses throughout their narratives to support their facts and enliven their tales.

Because the skalds' art was so highly respected, the names of poets were handed down with their verses. Some famous skalds even rated sagas of their own. *Egil's Saga,* written by Snorri Sturluson, tells the story of the tenth-century Icelander Egil Skalla-Grimsson. According to the saga, Egil was a swashbuckling poet,

A seventeenth-century Icelandic artist created this illustration of Egil Skalla-Grimsson, the hero of *Egil's Saga.*

The Power of Poetry

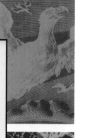

In *Egil's Saga,* Egil Skalla-Grimsson saves his life with a poem. Egil has been sentenced to death by King Erik Bloodaxe. The night before his execution, he composes a praise poem in Erik's honor. The flattered king grants the poet his "head as a present." Here are a few lines from the poem known as the "Head Ransom." You will notice that the poet uses kennings, including "scabbard-icicles" for "swords" and "Odin's forest of oaks" for "warriors."

The leader I laud,
sing surely his praise;
I ask to be heard,
an ode I can devise. . . .

Most men have learned
of the king's battle deeds
and the war-god saw
corpses strewn on the field. . . .

I heard they were felled,
Odin's forest of oaks,
by scabbard-icicles
in the play of iron. . . .

Yet more I desire
that men realize
his generous nature; . . .
he is worthy of praise.

warrior, farmer, and merchant whose adventures took him all over the Viking world.

Poems of Gods and Heroes

Another important group of poems from the Viking Age are the **Eddas.** Eddic poems are less complicated than skaldic verses. Their main subjects are the pagan gods and legendary heroes. Their composers are unknown.

After the Viking Age, thirty-four Eddic poems were written down in a collection called the *Elder Edda* or *Poetic Edda.* The first poem in the *Poetic Edda* describes the creation of the world and foretells its destruction in the great battle of Ragnarök.

Another well-known poem from the *Poetic Edda* is *Hávamál,* or "The Speech of the High One." *Hávamál* offers common-sense advice on everyday social conduct. It includes wise sayings for travelers, hosts, warriors, lovers, and friends. A number of tips relate to the proper behavior of guests in another man's hall.

> The tactful guest
> will take his leave
> early, not linger long;
> he starts to stink
> who outstays his welcome
> in a hall that is not his own.

The *Poetic Edda* was followed by a second collection known as the *Younger Edda* or *Prose Edda.* This handbook was written by Snorri Sturluson as a guide for young poets trying to master the complicated art of skaldic poetry. Since many of the kennings and other expressions in skaldic verse came from Scandinavian myths and legends, Snorri included a thorough account of the pagan gods and heroes. Much of his information was taken from the old Eddic poems.

The *Prose Edda* preserved many Eddic verses that might otherwise have been forgotten. It has also served as a valuable aid for modern-day scholars studying the Vikings' pagan beliefs and their complex, colorful poetry.

Snorri Sturluson was one of Scandinavia's most important poets and historians. Although he lived nearly two centuries after the Viking Age, his writings are a valuable source of information on those times.

Chapter VIII

SLAVES

The lowliest class in Viking society were the slaves, or **thralls.** No one knows their exact number. However, historians believe that thralls were common in Scandinavia and its colonies, because there are many references to slavery in Viking laws, the Icelandic sagas, and foreign chronicles.

Apart from these records, the thralls left few traces. In life, they were poor and powerless. When they died, their bodies were usually discarded without ceremony. The few remains of slaves have been discovered in the graves of much higher-ranking Vikings. One tenth-century burial pit in Denmark contained the skeletons of two men. The first had been laid to rest in a fine silk shirt, with a silver spear by his side. The second man was a slave who had been sacrificed to accompany his master to the afterworld. His feet were bound. From the odd position of his skull, archaeologists concluded that he had been beheaded.

The "Breed of Thralls"

Most thralls were foreigners captured in warfare or raids. The children born to these captives became slaves themselves. Free Vikings also might lose their freedom if they could not pay their debts or as a punishment for certain crimes.

Under the law, slaves were property. They could be bought and sold like farm animals. In fact, people were one of the

Speaking "Viking"

"Thrall," meaning "slave," is just one of many English words that came from the Old Norse language of the Vikings. Here are a few others: berserk, birth, fellow, freckle, glitter, husband, ill, kettle, kid, law, leg, outlaw, ransack, reindeer, rotten, skin, skull, sky, slaughter, squabble, starboard, steak, trust, ugly, walrus. In addition, our names for several days of the week come from Viking gods: Tuesday ("Tyr's Day"), Wednesday ("Woden's Day"), Thursday ("Thor's Day"), and Friday ("Freya's Day").

Viking slaves came from all over Europe. They performed a variety of tasks, including household duties such as preparing and serving meals.

Vikings' most profitable forms of "merchandise." According to several foreign writers, the Vikings traded slaves in lands all over eastern and western Europe. Around 1075, the German church chronicler Adam of Bremen observed that Danish slave raiders not only abducted "the barbarians who live around [the Baltic] sea" but also targeted their own countrymen. "As soon as one of them captures another," wrote the churchman, "he mercilessly sells him into slavery either to one of his fellows or to a barbarian."

Most slaves worked as household servants or farm laborers. They performed the hardest and dirtiest chores. According to the poem *Rigsthula,* the "breed of thralls" fathered by the wandering god Rig "laid fences, put dung on fields, fattened the swine, herded the goats, and grubbed up peat." Thralls also contributed much of the labor on forts and other large public building projects. Female slaves might be kept as concubines, forced to have sexual relations with their masters.

Slaves had few rights. They could not own land or speak in the assembly. They were not allowed to bear arms, except to fight off invaders. One law gave a slaveholder the right to injure or kill his thrall "unless he kills him during legally ordained festivals." A Viking who killed someone else's slave had to pay the owner compensation, just as he would for "any other cattle belonging to a man." In Iceland, the value of a thrall's life was set at 8 ounces (227 grams) of silver. In the Danelaw of England, it was the price of eight cows.

In pagan times, slaves were sometimes killed and buried with their masters. Arab traveler Ibn Fadlan witnessed the ritual sacrifice of a young female slave at the funeral of a Rus chieftain. The girl had volunteered to "die with her master." She may have believed that her choice would earn her an exalted place in the afterworld.

A Ritual Sacrifice

In 922, Ibn Fadlan watched as a slave girl in Russia was sacrificed aboard the burial ship of her master.

An old woman called the "Angel of Death" took hold of her head and made her enter the tent. The men began to beat their shields with wooden sticks, to stifle the cries of the slave girl. Two held her hands and two her feet, and the Angel of Death advanced with a broad-bladed dagger which she plunged repeatedly between the ribs of the girl while the men strangled her until she was dead. Then the closest relative of the dead man started a fire. The wood was engulfed in flames, then the ship, the tent and the man, the slave and everything in it.

The Price of Freedom

A thrall's life was not always entirely grim. Abusing a slave was considered bad behavior, and most owners seem to have treated their human property well. Slaves with special skills or beauty might live in comfort, enjoying a respected position in the household. A man could become an artisan or estate manager, while a woman might serve as governess to her owners' children.

Some owners allowed their slaves to earn income in their spare time, usually by farming a small patch of land or working in crafts. Thralls who worked hard might earn enough money to buy their freedom. A slave's freedom also could be bought by a friend or relative. Some slaves were eventually freed by their masters in reward for faithful service.

One way slaves could achieve their freedom was by earning money through the making and selling of crafts.

Ties of obligation bound freed slaves and their former owners for life. Freedmen were expected to ask for their masters' approval before marrying, moving, starting a new business, and all other major undertakings. The former owner was entitled to a share of any money the former slave won in a lawsuit or left to his heirs after death. In turn, the master owed the freedman support, guidance, and protection. In many parts of Scandinavia, masters formally adopted their freed slaves into their family.

One rune stone in Denmark bears witness to the lasting bond between slaves and their masters. This is the only memorial stone containing a record of slavery. It reads, "Toke the smith set up the stone in memory of Thorgisl, Gudmund's son, who gave him gold and freedom."

Chapter IX

THE LEGACY OF THE VIKINGS

By the eleventh century, the Viking world was changing. Christianity had taken hold in Scandinavia, uprooting old customs and ideals. Fewer young men were eager to go a-viking. It was easier to make a living in farming, business, or government, either at home or in one of the many settlements abroad. At the same time, plundering expeditions were becoming less profitable. After nearly three centuries of Viking raids, the kingdoms of Europe had built strong armies and fortifications to battle off invaders.

According to traditional histories, the Viking Age ended in 1066. In September of that year, King Harald Hardrada of Norway staged the last major Viking expedition. Assembling a fleet of three hundred warships, Harald invaded England, intent on seizing the throne. He and his warriors were annihilated by the army of English king Harold Godwinson. A few weeks later, an invasion force led by William the Conqueror of Normandy crushed the exhausted English army at the Battle

WILIAM · ·CONQVERO

William of Normandy conquered England in 1066, earning the name William the Conqueror. His rule marked the end of the Viking Age in western Europe.

of Hastings. On Christmas Day, the Norman leader was crowned king of England.

Under William's rule, French culture overshadowed Scandinavian influence in western Europe. Vikings who had settled overseas gradually adopted the language and customs of the local population, blending into the lands they had once terrorized. The Scandinavians' bold raids, explorations, and migrations dwindled. The tremendous energy and activity of the Viking Age faded away.

Although Vikings no longer sailed the seas, they had left traces that are still part of our world today. The adventurous Northmen changed the course of history in almost every region within reach of their longships. They built thriving cities in Russia. They settled Iceland, Greenland, and other islands in the North Atlantic. They founded Ireland's first towns and established the powerful French state of Normandy. The Vikings were also indirectly responsible for lasting political changes in Scotland and England. In each of these lands, repeated raiding weakened a number of rival groups struggling for dominance. That allowed a single group to rise to power and create a unified kingdom.

Another important legacy of the Vikings was their influence on law. Scandinavian settlers brought their justice system to the British Isles. In their administration of the Danelaw, accused criminals were judged by juries of twelve men who swore to decide all cases fairly and impartially. These courts were the ancestors of our modern jury system.

Today in Scandinavia, countless festivals, museums, and historical sites preserve the Viking legacy. The people of Norway, Denmark, Sweden, and Iceland look back proudly to the bold deeds and great achievements of their ancestors. A special source of pride are the Icelandic sagas. In these exciting tales of warriors

The Lord of the Rings

The Vikings' legacy has inspired many modern writers. Readers and movie fans may spot their influence in *The Hobbit* and *The Lord of the Rings* by J. R. R. Tolkien. Tolkien's heroes live according to Viking ideals of honor, courage, and fellowship. They write in runes. They preserve their history in poetry and song. Many other elements of Tolkien's stories were inspired by Scandinavian myths and legends, such as battling dwarfs and wizards, ancestral swords, and rings cursed with evil magic. The author even took some of his names for people and places from the Icelandic sagas. These include Gandalf, Thorin, Durin, Dain, Sauron, and Middle Earth.

and poets, feuds and battles, honor and glory, the Viking spirit lives on.

That extraordinary spirit may be the Vikings' most lasting legacy. The myths, legends, and ideals of the adventurous Northmen have inspired everything from cartoons and comic books to stirring operas and best-selling novels. American historian William Fitzhugh calls the Vikings "a kind of human myth come true." Their courage, creativity, and lust for adventure has inspired generations "to find new horizons, go new places, use new technology, meet new people, think new thoughts."

Norwegian raiders establish the town of Dublin, Ireland.

The army of King Halfdan of Denmark captures York, England.

A.D. **793**   **841**   C. **860**   **866**   C. **890**

Viking raiders attack the monastery of Lindisfarne, in England.

Viking explorers reach Iceland. Novgorod becomes the capital of a Viking kingdom in Russia.

Harald Fairhair wins the Battle of Hafrsfjord, uniting most of Norway under his rule.

Erik Bloodaxe becomes king of Norway.

Erik Bloodaxe becomes king of York.

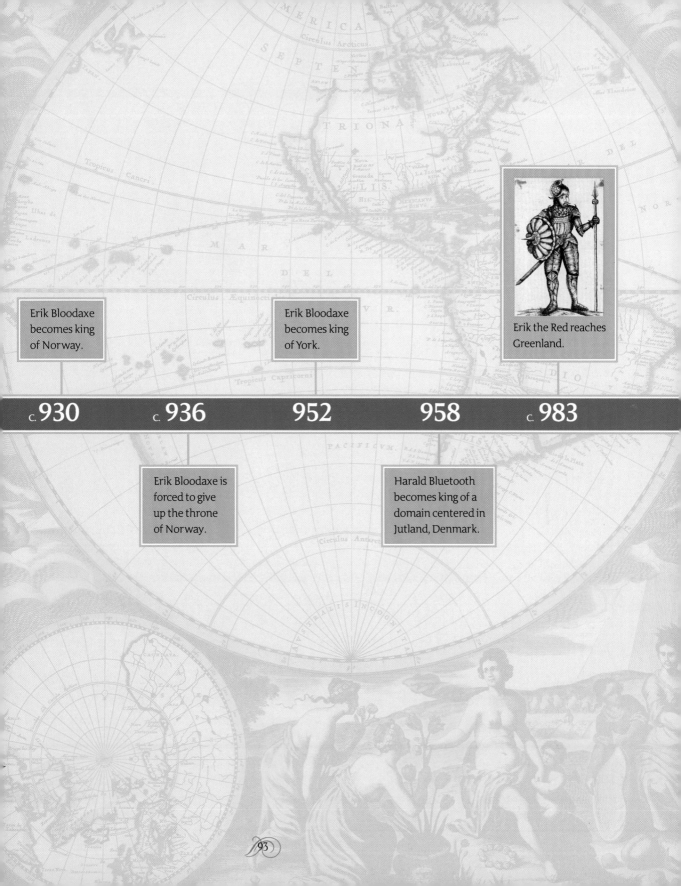

Erik the Red reaches Greenland.

c. 930   c. 936   952   958   c. 983

Erik Bloodaxe is forced to give up the throne of Norway.

Harald Bluetooth becomes king of a domain centered in Jutland, Denmark.

Viking forces led by Olaf Tryggvason defeat an English army near Maldon.

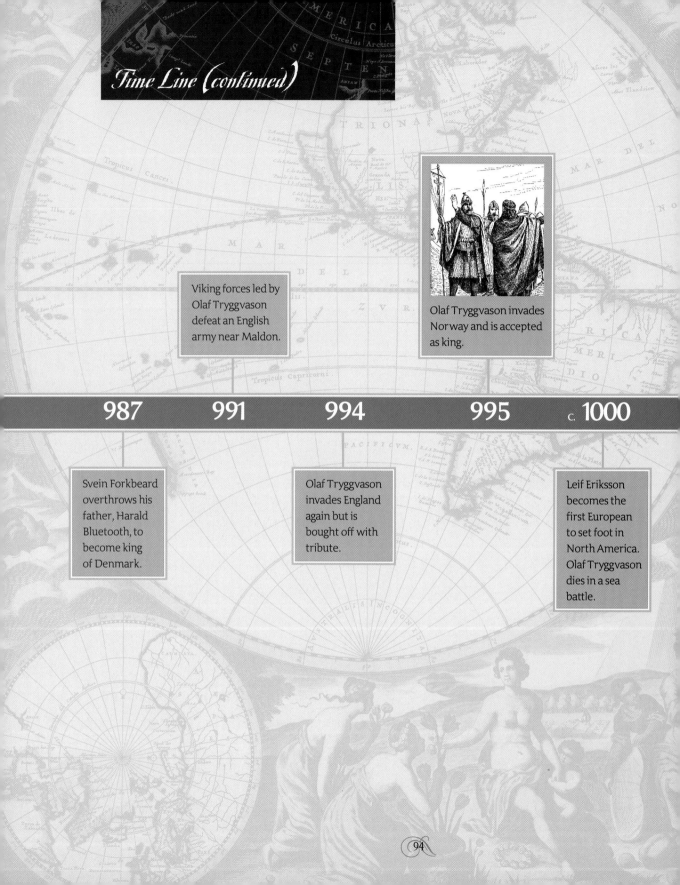

Olaf Tryggvason invades Norway and is accepted as king.

987   **991**   **994**   **995**   c. **1000**

Svein Forkbeard overthrows his father, Harald Bluetooth, to become king of Denmark.

Olaf Tryggvason invades England again but is bought off with tribute.

Leif Eriksson becomes the first European to set foot in North America. Olaf Tryggvason dies in a sea battle.

Svein Forkbeard conquers England.

Canute the Great becomes king of Denmark.

1013   **1017**   **1018**   **1066**

Canute the Great, son of Svein Forkbeard, becomes king of England.

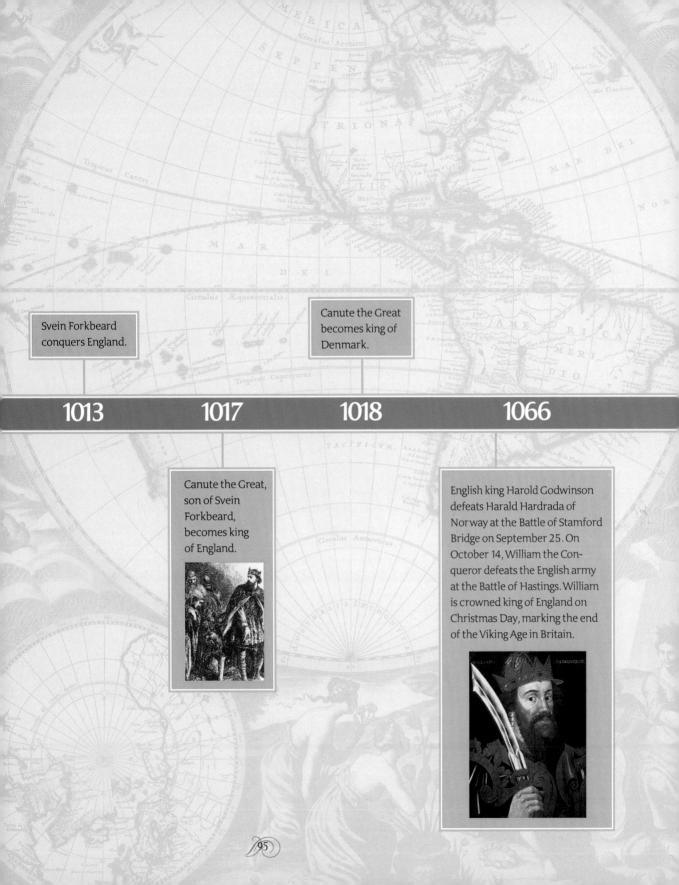

English king Harold Godwinson defeats Harald Hardrada of Norway at the Battle of Stamford Bridge on September 25. On October 14, William the Conqueror defeats the English army at the Battle of Hastings. William is crowned king of England on Christmas Day, marking the end of the Viking Age in Britain.

Canute the Great

Died 1035

Canute was the son of Danish king Svein Forkbeard. He took part in his father's conquest of England in 1013. After Svein's death, Canute established his rule over England, Denmark, Norway, and much of Sweden. He was known not only as a skilled military leader but also as a wise and just ruler.

Egil Skalla-Grimsson

Died c. 1000

Egil was a tenth-century Icelander and the hero of *Egil's Saga*, which was believed to have been written by Snorri Sturluson. The saga claims that Egil was a great poet, warrior, farmer, and merchant. Because he is not mentioned in any other source, it is impossible to tell how much of his story is true.

Erik Bloodaxe

Died 954

Erik was a king of Norway who killed several of his brothers to secure the throne following the death of his father, Harald Fairhair. A severe and unpopular ruler, he was expelled from Norway around 936. He went into exile and led several raids against England, briefly taking the throne of York.

Erik the Red

c. 950–1001

Erik the Red was a Viking adventurer who became the first European to explore Greenland. Around 983, he sailed west from Iceland and discovered the new land. Returning home, he persuaded other Icelanders to join him in colonizing Greenland.

Gorm the Old

Died 958

Gorm was a king of Denmark and the father of Harald Bluetooth. He was buried in a giant burial mound at Jelling.

Harald Bluetooth

Died 987

Harald Bluetooth was the first Christian king of Denmark. In 958, he succeeded his father, Gorm the Old, as ruler of a kingdom centered in the peninsula of Jutland. By the end of his reign, he had united all of Denmark under his rule. Harald died during a rebellion by his son Svein Forkbeard.

Harald Fairhair

c. 854-930

Harald Fairhair was the first king of a unified Norway. He defeated a coalition of minor kings and earls at the Battle of Hafrsfjord around 890, bringing most of the kingdom under his control.

Harald Hardrada

1015-1066

Norwegian king Harald Hardrada is sometimes called the last great Viking leader. He invaded England in 1066 and was killed in his army's defeat at the Battle of Stamford Bridge.

Harold Godwinson

c. 1020-1066

Harold Godwinson took the throne of England in 1066 and immediately faced challenges to his rule from both Harald Hardrada of Norway and William of Normandy. Harold was related through his mother to Canute the Great of Denmark.

Leif Eriksson

c. 975-1020

Leif Eriksson was a Viking explorer who is believed to be the first European to set foot in North America. Leif was intrigued by the stories of an Icelandic trader who claimed to have spotted a new land west of Greenland. He sailed across the North Atlantic and came to a unknown land that he named Vinland.

Magnus Barelegs

c. 1073-1103

Norwegian king Magnus Barelegs led some of the last Viking raids against the British Isles. His nickname came from his habit of wearing a Scottish kilt.

Olaf Tryggvason [OH-luf TRIG-vuh-sun]

c. 968-1000

Olaf Tryggvason grew up in exile from Norway, earning wealth and power as a leader of Viking raids. In 995, he invaded Norway and was accepted as king. After converting to Christianity, he used a combination of persuasion and violence to force his subjects to give up their pagan faith.

Olof Skötkonung

c. 995-1022

Olof was the first king known to have ruled the two major peoples of Sweden, the Götar and the Svear. He was also Sweden's first Christian king and the first to make coins and collect taxes. "Skötkonung" means "Tax King."

Saxo Grammaticus

c. 1150-1220

Denmark's earliest historian, Saxo Grammaticus wrote the sixteen-volume *Deeds of the Danes*, covering Danish history from legendary times to around the year 1200. The book is not considered a reliable history, but it is a good source of old myths, legends, songs, and poems.

Snorri Sturluson

c. 1179-1271

Snorri Sturluson was an Icelandic statesman, poet, and historian whose writings are an important source of information on the Viking Age. His best-known works include *Heimskringla*, a collection of sagas on the lives of Norway's Viking kings, and the *Prose Edda*, a handbook of Scandinavian poetry and mythology.

Svein Forkbeard

Died 1014

Svein Forkbeard became king of Denmark in 987, after seizing power from his father, Harald Bluetooth. Svein led a series of raids against England, ending in its conquest in 1013. He was king of England for only a few weeks before he fell ill and died.

Thorvi

Died c. 950

The wife of Denmark's King Gorm and mother of Harald Bluetooth, Thorvi is known mainly from memorials raised to her at Jelling. Her burial mound was plundered long ago, and her body has never been found.

William the Conqueror

c. 1027-1087

William the Conqueror was a Norman leader who defeated the English army at the Battle of Hastings and was crowned king of England in 1066. He was a descendant of Viking raiders who had settled in Normandy in France. However, he and his followers were Frenchmen at heart, and his rule brought an end to the Viking Age in Britain.

adornment Something that decorates or beautifies

amber A gold-colored substance that comes from the fossilized resin of trees. The Vikings carved and polished amber into beads, pendants, game pieces, and other prized objects.

Anglo-Saxon Chronicle A collection of texts recording England's history from the fifth to mid-twelfth centuries. The *Anglo-Saxon Chronicle* is an important source of information on Viking raids and conquests in England.

archaeologists Scientists who study the physical remains of past cultures to learn about human life and activity

artifacts Objects from a particular period of history

bartering The act of carrying out a trade by exchanging one item for another, instead of selling the goods for money

berserkers A special group of Viking warriors who were famous for their wild, ferocious style of fighting. The word "berserker" means "bear shirt" and may have come from the fighters' bearskin cloaks.

dendrochronology (den-droh-kruh-NAH-luh-jee) The science of dating wooden objects from their patterns of growth rings. By examining living trees, scientists have created "calendars" of growth rings for trees in different areas of the world, dating back thousands of years. They use the calendars to date pieces of wood from those areas.

Eddas Scandinavian poems written in a simpler style than skaldic verse, usually dealing with the pagan gods and legendary heroes

félag A fellowship of Viking men who joined together to share the costs, responsibilities, and profits of an enterprise such as a raiding or trading expedition. The members of the félag owed loyalty to one another and to the group's leader.

freemen The Viking social class that included all free adult men. Most freemen were farmers, craftspeople, or merchants.

futhark (FOO-thark) The runic alphabet of the Scandinavians. The word comes from the sounds of the first six runes (*f, u, th, a, r, k*).

hacksilver Fragments chopped from silver jewelry, coins, and other items, which the Vikings used to pay for goods

heathens Uncivilized people, especially those who do not believe in the God of the Bible. "Heathen" was one of the names the English used for the Vikings.

Hebrides A group of islands in the Atlantic Ocean, off the west coast of Scotland

inscriptions Words written or engraved in stone, metal, or some other hard surface

jarls [yarls] The wealthiest and most powerful men of the Viking upper class. In English, jarl means "earl."

kennings Two-part metaphors used in skaldic poems in place of common words. For example, a poet might say "bone rain" for "blood" or "ship's road" for "sea."

leaf-knives Viking farm tools used to cut cereals or hay for animal feed. A leaf-knife looked like a long, sharp knife with a curving hook at one end.

lid The personal band of warriors attached to a Viking king or chieftain

longhouse A long, narrow Viking farmhouse. The longhouse was divided into several rooms, with a barn for livestock at one end.

longships Long, narrow Viking ships that were used mainly for raiding and warfare. Longships usually had a single sail and a long row of oars on each side.

mead A sweet alcoholic beverage made from honey, water, grain, and yeast

mercenaries Professional soldiers who serve in an army for pay

monasteries Places where monks (men who belong to a religious order) live and work apart from the rest of the world

pagans People who worship many different gods and goddesses

panpipes A simple wind instrument made by binding together small wooden pipes of different lengths

plunder To steal goods or take them by force during raids or warfare. "Plunder" can also mean the goods that are taken.

pyre A pile of flammable materials for burning a dead body as part of a funeral rite

Ragnarök (RAG-nuh-ruhk) In Scandinavian mythology, the final battle between the gods and giants that would bring about the destruction of the world. "Ragnarök" means "Doom of the Gods."

rudder A flat piece of wood or metal used for steering a ship

runes Letters in an ancient alphabet used by a number of Germanic peoples, including the Vikings

sagas Long tales written in Iceland during the thirteenth and early fourteenth centuries, which were often about historical and legendary heroes of the Viking Age

scythes (siethz) Farm tools consisting of a long curving blade attached to a long handle, used for harvesting grain

sickles Harvesting tools consisting of a short curving blade attached to a short handle

skalds Poets who composed verses honoring the kings and chieftains. These verses were recited at feasts and other public gatherings.

soapstone A type of soft stone that is abundant in Scandinavia, which the Vikings carved into bowls, cooking pots, lamps, sculptures, and other goods

tapestries Heavy cloths woven with complicated scenes or designs, which are used as wall hangings

tempered Strengthened tools or other metal objects, often by heating and then cooling them

tenant farmers Farmers who work land that is owned by someone else, often paying rent with a portion of their harvest

Things The assemblies of freemen that formed the basis of Viking government. The Things were responsible for making laws and judging legal cases.

thralls Viking slaves. The word means "unfree servant."

tribute A payment given by one ruler or country to another as a sign of respect and submission

turf Mats of soil bound together by grass and plant roots, which were used like bricks for building. Turf houses may also be called sod houses.

Valhalla The great hall of the god Odin, where the souls of heroic Viking warriors were believed to dwell after death. "Valhalla" means "hall of the slain."

Valkyries (val-KIR-eez) Mythical maiden warriors who were believed to live with the god Odin and guide the souls of fallen heroes to his paradise in Valhalla

wattle and daub A framework of woven twigs and branches plastered with clay or mud, used as a building material

Books

Gallagher, Jim. *The Viking Explorers.* Explorers of New Worlds series. Philadelphia: Chelsea House, 2001.

Grant, Neil. *The Vikings.* Spotlights series. New York: Oxford University Press, 1998.

Gravett, Christopher. *Going to War in Viking Times.* Armies of the Past series. Danbury, CT: Franklin Watts, 2001.

Guy, John. *Viking Life.* Early Civilizations series. Hauppauge, NY: Barron's Educational Series, 1998.

Hinds, Kathryn. *The Vikings.* Cultures of the Past series. New York: Marshall Cavendish, 1998.

Lassieur, Allison. *The Vikings.* Lost Civilizations series. San Diego, CA: Lucent Books, 2001.

Rees, Rosemary. *The Vikings.* Understanding People in the Past series. Chicago, IL: Heinemann Library, 2002.

Organizations and Online Sites

Artefacts Alive! Jorvik: The Viking City
http://www.yorkarchaeology.co.uk/artefacts/start.htm

Archeologists have re-created the Viking city of Jorvik (York, England), offering visitors a vivid picture of town life one thousand years ago. Visit the Web site for a behind-the-scenes look at the artifacts discovered at York and how scientists have worked to bring them to life.

BBCi History: Vikings
http://www.bbc.co.uk/history/ancient/vikings

This terrific site from the British Broadcasting Corporation offers lots of information on warfare, religion, food, family life, and many other aspects of Viking history and culture. Visit the "Multimedia Zone" for interactive games, animations, and tours of reconstructed historical sites.

Canadian Museum of Civilization
100 Laurier Street
P. O. Box 3100, Station B
Gatineau, QC, Canada J8X 442
http://www.civilization.ca/hist/canp1/ca01eng.html

The Canada Hall at the Canadian Museum of Civilization re-creates sights and sounds from the country's past, beginning with the arrival of Norse explorers. The Web site offers lots of information about Viking ships and the everyday life of Viking settlers in North America.

Compass
http://www.thebritishmuseum.ac.uk/compass

Type in "Vikings" on this site's "Quick Search" engine, and you will find photos of the British Museum's many Viking Age artifacts, including coins, weapons, and jewelry. There are also links to pages with information on warfare, trade, and settlement.

Encyclopedia Mythica: Norse Mythology
http://www.pantheon.org/areas/mythology/europe/norse/articles.html

This site offers a listing of nearly 150 articles on Norse gods and myths.

The Metropolitan Museum of Art
1000 Fifth Avenue
New York, NY 10028-0198
http://www.metmuseum.org/toah/hd/vikg/hd_vikg.htm

The Metropolitan Museum's Timeline of Art History includes photos and descriptions of items from the museum's collection of Viking art and weapons.

National Museum of Natural History
Smithsonian Institution
10th Street and Constitution Avenue, N.W.
Washington, DC 20560
http://www.mnh.si.edu/vikings

The Smithsonian's exhibit "Vikings: The North Atlantic Saga" explores the origins and impact of Leif Eriksson's arrival in North America one thousand years ago. The museum's Web site includes examples of artifacts from the exhibit, plus information on Viking history and archaeological finds.

NOVA Online: The Vikings
http://www.pbs.org/wgbh/nova/vikings

At this companion Web site to the NOVA program *The Vikings,* you can explore a Viking village, learn the secrets of Norse ships, and write your name in runes.

About the Author

Virginia Schomp has written more than fifty titles for young readers on topics including dolphins, dinosaurs, occupations, American history, and world history. Her books on cultures of the past include three other titles in the People of the Ancient World series: *The Ancient Chinese, Ancient Mesopotamia,* and *Ancient India.* She is most intrigued by the "story" in history—the writings and artifacts that bring alive the beliefs, struggles, hopes, and dreams of people who lived long ago. Her favorite part of researching *The Vikings* was discovering the real men and women behind the legends. When we look beneath the traditional image of bloodthirsty, axe-wielding barbarians, we find mothers and fathers, wives and husbands, hardworking farmers and bold adventurers who sailed the seas in search of riches and glory.

Ms. Schomp earned a Bachelor of Arts degree in English Literature from the Pennsylvania State University. She lives in the Catskill Mountain region of New York.